Derek Hairon

SIT-ON-TOP
KAYAK

A BEGINNER'S MANUAL

First published in Great Britain 2007 by Pesda Press
Unit 22, Galeri
Doc Victoria
Caernarfon
Gwynedd
LL55 1SQ

Reprinted 2009

ISBN: 978-1-906095-02-4

Printed and bound in Poland. www.polskabook.pl

THE AUTHOR

Derek Hairon

British Canoe Union Level 5 Sea Kayak Coach and Director of Jersey Kayak Adventures Ltd, one of the leading specialist sit-on-top kayak outfitters in the United Kingdom.

Derek has kayaked for over forty years. He first learned to kayak around the incredible coastline of Jersey in the Channel Islands (which has some of the largest tides in the world) after his father built him a sit-on-top kayak. He has undertaken many kayak expeditions, most notably a circumnavigation of Ireland in fifty-eight days and expeditions to Alaska, Canada, as well as whitewater kayaking in Nepal. Closer to home he has paddled extensively in the Channel Islands including thirty-five mile open crossings. He has kayaked most of the best coastal spots in the UK.

In his younger days he was a member of the Jersey surf kayak team and has been active in coaching sea kayaking in Jersey. Active in other sports too, he undertook a 12,000 mile cycle tour in 1984 and also is a keen skier and walker.

In 2004 he set up Jersey Kayak Adventures to offer tours and courses to cater for the growth in this popular sport.

ACKNOWLEDGEMENTS

Oh boy. Just who do you thank?

I guess Gary Kemp, formidable surf kayaker and sea paddler and co-Director of Jersey Kayak Adventures Ltd, for helping to develop our approach to kayaking. Kath Nicolson for proofreading the drafts. Krista and Nicholas Hairon for lots of background work and help. Renee Taraud for support, especially when the hard drive failed as the final draft was being prepared for sending to the editor. Then there are all the kayaking coaches and paddlers I have had the pleasure of kayaking with over the years, especially in the Jersey Canoe Club which seems to be a breeding ground for some great sea kayakers who simply get out and get paddling in waters that sometimes would scare the pants off me. When getting trashed in a serious rock hop full of whitewater and crashing surf it is always good to know others of similar ability are around to lend a hand and to help push my limits even further.

And then there is my Dad, Ack Hairon, who along with my kayak coach David Thelland helped start all this many years ago. If Mum had quite realised what Dad was getting up to on his kayak I doubt if she would have let me near one.

Finally, thanks to lots of clients on our courses who sometimes found themselves being the test bed for ideas.

Thank you to all those who have contributed photographs including; Bob Campbell, Rob Jones, Scotty, Ocean Kayak, Gumotex, Valley, Lendal, Bic Sport, Crewsaver, Robson, Feelfree, Aquapac, Emotion, Palm and Wilderness Systems.

CONTENTS

What can you do with a sit-on-top? You can surf, rock-hop, bird-watch, fish, dive, go camping and explore all with the same single kayak – and the same kayak can be used for all the family.

WHY CHOOSE A SIT-ON-TOP KAYAK?

Sit-on-top kayaking is fun. It is the fastest growing paddlesport for this simple reason.

It is accessible to almost anybody who has a desire to experience nature and the outdoors. Anyone of average fitness can take part, there are many adaptations available for those with special needs, and age is not a big factor. You just need an open mind and to be willing to explore and discover our fantastic aquatic environment that is not easily reached by other craft.

Sit-on-top kayaks are the big development in paddlesport. Built in affordable modern plastics, they are durable and come in all shapes and sizes to suit different needs. Learning is rapid and you can pick up all the basics very quickly.

Sit-on-tops enable people to get afloat without fear of capsizing (you will simply fall off into the water). These versatile craft are designed to be stable and user friendly in many situations, from messing about with the family on a lake, fishing your favourite deep water spot, or exploring a rocky coastline.

Relatively easy to transport, a sit-on-top can be launched in almost any spot with much less hassle than moving a small dinghy.

Paddling is a social experience too. When you paddle with others you can choose how far you wish to go, and what you would rather not do; as you watch a paddler slipping into a cave you are part of the shared experience. You can explore and discover, on your own terms, places that other small craft can rarely get to.

Kayaking requires just enough concentration to enable the stress and everyday activities of our busy lives to be forgotten. It is a chance to 'decompress' and for a few hours to become an adventurer in a changing and often magical environment.

WHERE CAN YOU PADDLE?

You can get up-to-date information on the changing situation of access from national governing bodies such as the British Canoe Union or the Inland Waterways Authority.

It would be nice to be able to go afloat anywhere you see water. However, things are not so simple. It is important to judge for yourself the water and weather conditions, and also to ensure that you have the right of access to your planned launching and landing sites. Some waters may have exclusion zones (such as military firing ranges or nature reserves) and in other places land-owners may not allow public access.

Rivers

The force of moving water should never be underestimated, so read the sections that cover safety on rivers with care. Forewarned is forearmed.

Rivers, whether fast flowing in their upland stretches or lazy and meandering in the lowlands, give you a unique perspective on the countryside and its wildlife as you drift downstream.

Major rivers flow all year round. Larger rivers, particularly in their lower reaches become busy shipping navigations, and are often popular with other river users such as sailing and rowing clubs.

Throughout the world many rivers run wild, although there may be localised restrictions on boating in special cases such as drinking water catchment areas. Continental Europe has sharing arrange-ments for river use, with evenings given over to fishing from the banks, so try and find out what the local arrangements are.

The best bet is to check with local kayak shops or canoe clubs to find out what the local situation is, or consult the BCU website.

The situation in England and Wales is less enlightened, where people are less likely to be willing to share the riverside. Many of the larger rivers such as the Thames, the Trent and the Severn require a British Waterways licence (included in British Canoe Union membership). On other rivers your right of navigation may be contested by land-owners.

> **JOIN YOUR NATIONAL CANOE SPORT ASSOCIATION (SUCH AS THE BRITISH CANOE UNION). YOU'LL GET LOTS OF INFORMATION ON WHERE TO PADDLE AND WHICH KAYAK CLUBS ARE IN YOUR AREA. YOUR SUBSCRIPTION MAY ALSO HELP THE CAMPAIGN FOR BETTER ACCESS TO RIVERS, LAKES AND THE COAST. SEE PAGE 88 FOR DETAILS.**

Canals

Look out for other craft and sunken or floating junk. Water quality is likely to be poor, so don't swim in the canal.

Canal Locks are not suitable for kayaks and you will need to carry your boat around them (portage) on the tow path.

Canals were the arteries of the industrial revolution in the 18th and 19th century. As such they run through the heart of many historic towns and cities. They provide safe and quiet passage through miles of countryside; interrupted only by the locks that punctuate the length of a canal to allow progress uphill.

The waterways licence included in the British Canoe Union membership package covers the entire British canal network. Their still and calm water can be a great place to discover kayaking.

Lakes

Deep water lakes can be very cold once you leave the shallows.

Lakes have varied characteristics and origins. They could be deep water lakes in dramatic glacial valleys, shallow ox-bow lakes separated from the meander of the river, or man-made lakes such as disused gravel pits. The same access considerations that apply to rivers also apply to lakes. Working gravel pits and quarries will be off limits for obvious safety reasons.

On larger lakes wind and waves may make paddling difficult. It is usually possible to launch at the sheltered end of the lake on a windy day. On small lakes the wind will blow you to the shore if you bite off more than you can chew.

The sea

The sea is perhaps the most popular destination for sit-on-top kayaking. It is, in suitable conditions, a wonderful playground... but it must always be treated with respect. Tides, currents and the effect of wind can change a seemingly safe coastline into a maelstrom of waves. Books such as *Sea Kayak Navigation* provide basic information about the effects of wind and tides.

Avoid large and busy harbours. Ferries, yachts and power boats can appear from all directions and you will not be easily spotted by them.

Access is not usually an issue, the biggest problem may be finding a place to park. Never obstruct slipways and harbour areas in case emergency craft need to go afloat. Driving vehicles onto beaches will one day lead to you getting stuck in the sand or mud and usually it will be when the tide is rising. Use a **kayak trolley** (see page 31) instead of driving onto the beach.

Some busy beaches may be 'zoned' for bathers, surfers and other water users. Paddle within the areas signposted for watercraft.

Wildlife is one of the great attractions of paddling on the sea. However, some areas are particularly sensitive, such as sand dunes, feeding areas in estuaries and lagoons, and roosting and nesting sites on cliffs. Do your best to find out about and comply with any local restrictions or codes of conduct.

GETTING STARTED

See page 88 for some good wesbites and useful contacts to help get you started.

If you're not already sitting in your kayak, on the water, reading this book, there are a few things which may be worth considering or trying out before you take the plunge.

Buy or hire?

A growing number of outdoor centres offer tours and courses. Look for outdoor activity or watersports centres.

Before rushing out to buy a sit-on-top it is worth considering just how often you are likely to use the kayak and all the equipment. For the occasional user, it may well be better to hire from an outfitter or sign up to a course or a kayak tour where all the gear will be supplied. You'll get to use quality equipment and go on trips you might not otherwise have undertaken. You won't have to drive with your kayak on your car and you won't have to make space to store your kayak at home. Best of all, at the end of the trip you leave someone else to wash and sort out all the gear.

Get tuition

Tuition and courses will also put you in touch with other kayakers to paddle with.

Learning from your own experience is invaluable, but you may end up learning poor technique, buying the wrong equipment, or progressing slowly. Signing up for a sit-on-top kayaking course will enable you to learn good technique and to paddle safely.

Transport and storage

Moving the kayak

Most paddling related back injuries happen when moving kayaks. This could be at the beach or just as often in your own back yard. See the section on 'Lifting and carrying' (page 31) before grappling with your kayak.

Storing your kayak outside

Keep the kayak out of direct sunlight as some brands do lose their colour over time. In most cases the problem of the plastic becoming brittle due to exposure to the sun has been largely eradicated thanks to UV inhibitors added to modern plastics. Consider how you will secure the kayak to reduce the risk of theft. A chain run through the drain holes should deter opportunist thieves.

Vertical storage saves space. Make sure that whatever you tie or padlock your kayak to is strong enough.

Detachable roof rack roller.

Roof racks

Check out the cost of a roof rack for the car and whether your vehicle can accommodate a rack. Roof racks can be expensive options. If you use upright bars, remember to allow for your extra vehicle height when entering car parks.

A small trailer can be an excellent alternative. This eliminates the need to lift the kayak onto a car roof and lessens the risk of damage to your car. After paddling, your wet kit and clothing can be stored in the trailer box, keeping your car dry.

Due mainly to weight restrictions, two kayaks is usually the limit on a roof rack.

A detachable roof mounted roller can help make it easier to load a kayak onto a car roof rack.

Straps are easy to use and don't require you to learn complicated knots. Ropes are more versatile.

Putting a twist in the straps can stop them from humming when driving. Threading the straps through any convenient strong points is also a good idea.

Kayaks and paddles must be well secured when travelling. On any journey tie the kayak at both the bow and stern and also laterally across the roof rack. Do not use elastic bungee style cords, as these can detach suddenly. Use rope or straps and check that the weight limits for your roof rack are adhered to.

If you have a large amount of boat overhanging the front or back of your vehicle then you must ensure the overhang is clearly marked with a red marker or flag. Outside the UK, the law may require lighting and reflective boards.

⚠ DON'T CUT CORNERS WHEN TYING YOUR BOAT ON. THE EXPERIENCE OF A KAYAK OR PADDLES DETACHING FROM A ROOF RACK AT HIGH SPEED IS HORRENDOUS AND LIFE-THREATENING.

Choosing a kayak

Sit-on-tops come in a bewildering range of designs and sizes. Like buying a car there is not one design that suits all requirements. A little time spent thinking about what you plan to do with the kayak and who will use it can save you from buying something inappropriate. Try them out before you buy. What initially feels re-assuringly stable may, after a few trips, seem like a cumbersome barge as your skills improve.

One kayak can do it all, but some are better for fishing, fun, family or surfing.

THE LONG AND SHORT OF IT

Long, narrow kayaks will go in straighter lines and are better for touring and paddling distances. Shorter kayaks are more manoeuvrable and responsive; they are fun in surf and moving water and for nipping around rocks. Wider kayaks are more stable. They can be good platforms for fishing and other activities but are more sluggish and less responsive.

2m

1m

THE PADDLER

You also need to bear in mind that paddlers also come in different sizes, builds and ages. What may for one person be an ideal kayak to surf and play will be uncomfortable for another to paddle any distance or cast a fishing line from. Seats may be too large for a small child or there might be extra storage wells in which a toddler or pet could sit.

Narrow your choice down to a few designs. If possible try them out afloat. If you think you may be using the kayak to fish or for longer trips then some storage space will be useful.

Inflatables

A big problem is that they are relatively light and therefore float high on the water. They are more prone to the effects of wind and can become hard to paddle in even moderate winds.

Inflatable sit-on-tops have proved themselves to be ideal craft for anyone who is planning to travel into remote areas where it might otherwise be very hard to transport a rigid kayak. For anyone with very limited storage space an inflatable has definite advantages.

The down side is that you get what you pay for and well-designed inflatables tend to be quite expensive. They also puncture more easily and suffer from the effects of abrasion, though a good quality inflatable will allow you to make repairs.

Essentials

Along with a sit-on-top and paddles (see Paddles on page 17), you'll need at least a buoyancy aid (see Flotation on page 27) and clothing appropriate to the environment (from a bathing suit to a wetsuit, woolly hat and windproof – see Clothing on page 22). Other items might also be advisable, depending on the type of paddling you intend to do...

EQUIPMENT AND ACCESSORIES

As optional accessories to your sit-on-top kayak there will often be a seat and back rest system available as well as thigh straps and rudder options.

Back rests and seats

Seats and back supports come in various designs. Whether the support includes a padded seat is optional.

Back and upper body support is essential to developing good technique and allows you to use larger muscle groups when paddling. It also reduces fatigue.

A good upright sitting position is acheived when the base of the spine is in contact with the lower part of the back rest. The rest of the spine is supported but mobility is not restricted.

Thigh straps

Thigh straps can give extra control when making turns and other manoeuvres. In rough water and surf they allow you to be in full control of the kayak.

Thigh straps can be used when needed. Most photos in this book do not show thigh straps in use, as many people find them restrictive and they are simply an additional complication.

Rudders

Some love them and some hate them. They are usually sold as an optional extra fitted to your kayak (but kits are also available).

On the plus side, a rudder allows more of your forward paddling effort to be used to move you where you want to go without worrying about steering strokes.

In following seas (where the wind and waves are coming from behind) a rudder can come into its own; counteracting the turning effect of the wind to stay pointing ahead. Changing your paddle grip can also help (see page 37).

The down side is that you may come to rely on your rudder. If you learn good techniques without a rudder, you will use a rudder even more effectively. If faced with rudder failure you can still control your kayak. A good kayak will work with or without the use of a rudder.

If you opt for a rudder system, choose carefully. Some rudder systems are more suited to sprint racing and are not so strong. It is easy to underestimate the strain rudder systems can be placed under. Fittings need to be both strong, repairable and allow the rudder to be taken out of use if a problem develops.

It's just a paddle isn't it? No, it's a 210cm 70° right-hand feathered asymmetric touring paddle.

Paddles

I often still see kayakers with great kayaks and paddles little better than a pair of shovels bought from the local hardware store thrown in as a free item at the end of a sale.

Once upon a time selecting paddles was pretty easy. A bit of ply-wood and some round dowelling hacked into something vaguely resembling a pair of spades. Length was assessed by standing the paddle vertically and with your arm raised checking if the knuckles could curl around the top of the blade. Then you went kayaking. Fortunately we have moved on with highly efficient designs. Paddles are our sole means of propulsion, so you should make your selection carefully.

Paddle length

Paddles come in different lengths to suit your height, the type of kayak you use and the conditions you will paddle in. It is therefore important to have an idea of what you want to do with the kayak and the sort of paddler you are.

For touring a longer paddle length is recommended as it allows a slower rate. However, if the paddle is too long for your build it will be difficult to rapidly change your paddle speed. Many touring kayakers and shorter paddlers tend to use paddles which are slightly too long for them. If possible try a range of lengths before making a decision.

If you do a lot of different types of kayaking then you may need to consider not just a different kayak but also different paddles. For whitewater or surf, paddles between 1.8m and 2m are often used. For touring a longer length of between 2m and 2.2m might be used. Your preference and paddling style is a big factor.

Below – a rough guide to assessing length – you should be just able to curl your fingertips over the top of the paddle. For surfing, where you need to be able to swing the paddle quickly into different positions, a shorter paddle would be better.

BLADE SHAPE

Symmetric blades reduce blade wobble in the water. They respond the same whichever way the paddle is held, which can be helpful in rough water.

Asymmetric paddle blades have less surface area below the line of the shaft. The whole blade comes under equal pressure, which produces a more efficient paddle stroke. Avoid paddling with the blades upside down (with the shorter edge uppermost). This is less efficient and wrecks your kayaking credibility!

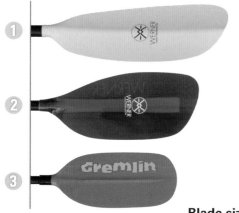

1 low angle asymmetric paddle.

2 high angle asymmetric paddle.

3 high angle symmetric child's paddle (with smaller blade area and thinner shaft).

Blade designs can make a considerable difference to your paddle style. Paddles designed for smaller people have less blade area. This develops better technique and reduces the risk of injury.

Blade size

Paddle blades come in different sizes to suit build and physique. Larger blades are appropriate for stronger paddlers. Many paddlers of smaller build wrongly believe that big paddle blades will enable them to paddle quicker and keep up with the others. A smaller paddle blade will often allow a faster paddle rate. This can give you the same speed but with less exertion. It also allows you to rapidly alter your speed.

High or low angle paddling

These terms describe whether your paddle style is a high action (usually the top arm is seen above shoulder height), or low angle (the arm is below shoulder height).

The left kayaker is paddling with a high action style and the right kayaker is using a low action.

High angle blades are often recommended for kayakers who paddle at a faster rate or use a larger range of paddle strokes in challenging conditions. Low angle paddle blades are more stretched in length. This is reputed to favour a touring and relaxed style of kayaking.

High angle entry encourages a good paddle style. The height of the top arm can be raised or lowered to suit conditions.

The distinction between high and low angle styles is often an excuse for poor technique. While there is nothing wrong with either blade design, far too many low angle paddlers have slipped into this low style as a result of habit. A high action paddle style can be lowered in rough conditions or when you are tired, but a permanently low angle style reduces your repertoire of techniques. Practise an efficient high action paddle stroke.

Blade angle

From left to right, blades set at 0°, 45° and 65°.

When paddles are set at angles this is known as 'feather'. Straight set paddles are called 'unfeathered'. Though unfeathered paddles initially seem easier to use they result in a less comfortable wrist action. Paddles are often set at angles between 45–70°. Blade angles of around 65° are often a good starting point. Many manufacturers now produce jointed paddles that allow blade angles to be adjusted until you find a comfortable angle.

WHEN CHOOSING ANY PADDLE SHAPE OTHER THAN A FLAT BLADE IT IS IMPORTANT TO CHECK IF IT IS SET FOR LEFT-HANDED OR RIGHT-HANDED USE.

Paddle shafts

Paddles are often sold in a range of specifications 'off the peg'. A good kayak shop can also build you a bespoke paddle.

Paddle shafts are available in different diameters to suit your hand size. If your hands do not fit comfortably around the shaft it indicates that you need a smaller or larger diameter shaft. This helps to reduce fatigue.

A 'split' shaft will allow you to break down your paddle into two or more pieces for storage. More advanced split shafts such as the Lendal Varilock allow the paddle to be reassembled at various lengths and feathers – great for tired wrists, group use or simply trying out the range of possibilities.

Look for a paddle shaft that is ovalised at the places where your hands should grip, or that has grips shrink wrapped to the shaft. The grip position is often called the 'index' and helps your wrists comfortably align with the blade angle.

Bent or cranked shafts are more expensive. A straight shaft has the advantage of being cheaper and lighter. They are also easier to move your hand along to use the paddle in an extended position.

A bent (cranked) paddle shaft with ergonomic grip position.

Paddle leashes

Paddle leashes provide a good method of keeping your paddle with you in case of a capsize or if you hit rough water. A secure and easy-to-attach small snap shackle (as in the photo below) will make it easy to clip and unclip the paddle. Some plastic shackles can open unexpectedly causing the paddle to become detached and leave you up the creek without a paddle.

I often use elasticated 'shock cord' as this lets me use a short leash that can still give plenty of movement. If you do use shock cord make sure that it is securely attached to the kayak and shackle as knots can become loose in elastic.

CLOTHING AND FLOTATION

The correct clothing afloat is essential for your comfort and safety. The difficulty is that the weather and temperature can vary tremendously from day to day and hour to hour.

While many items of kit can be worn by a range of builds, most kayak manufacturers produce a range of garments designed to give maximum comfort and enjoyment afloat.

Always try to wear the correct size of clothing suitable for your age, weight, build and gender. Wearing badly fitting clothing, especially for young people, can be a big turn-off.

Water temperature

Our bodies need to remain at a constant temperature of 37°C. If our inner body temperature is allowed to fall then we are likely to become clumsy, disorientated and unable to follow instructions. Unchecked this can kill. Many water-based tragedies are caused not by drowning but by hypothermia.

Even during the hottest summers the water temperature rarely reaches above 17°C in the English Channel and Channel Islands. On lakes and rivers water temperature can be very low once you move away from the shallows. If you are immersed for any length of time your chances of survival will not be more than a few hours without some form of protective clothing.

We are not as well prepared as others for cold water.

©iStockphoto.com Wolfgang Schoenfeld

⚠ HYPOTHERMIA CAN EASILY GO UNNOTICED IN THE EARLY STAGES. SUITABLE CLOTHING IS VITAL TO ENSURE NOT ONLY YOUR ENJOYMENT AND COMFORT BUT ALSO TO KEEP YOU SAFE.

Wind chill

Even on a warm day, the moment the wind starts blowing it feels cooler. Pack or wear appropriate clothing for the temperatures and remember that it will be cooler afloat.

What to wear

What you wear will be influenced by the weather forecast for the day and your own levels of comfort. A simple rule is to always wear a little more than you think you need. Wear many thinner layers rather than one or two thick layers (this enables you to adjust the number of layers to stay comfortable). Carry extra clothing so that you can put it on as soon as you (or others) start to feel cold. If you are fishing, then allow for the fact that after paddling to your fishing spot you will not be moving about as much.

1 *A long john style wetsuit provides good all round comfort. A rash vest or thermal base layer worn between your body and the wetsuit will provide more warmth and be more comfortable.*

2 *A thermal base layer and board shorts will often be the most comfortable option on warm days, unless you take a dunking.*

3 *Adding a cagoule / paddle jacket over your wetsuit or thermals is a good way to greatly reduce wind chill.*

Wetsuits

Wetsuit manufacturers produce specific children's and women's fit wetsuits. The larger paddler will find XXL and XXXL sizes available for most items of kit including buoyancy aids.

A shortie wetsuit is good single layer solution for warmer days (short legs and arms). Be sure to protect yourself from the sun.

For the sit-on-top kayaker this offers some of the best protection when paddling. For summer use, a 3mm thickness is often adequate and extra comfort can be obtained by combining this with a fleece top. In cooler conditions a thicker wetsuit is useful but can be restrictive. Other types of protective clothing, such as dry tops and trousers or full dry suits, may offer better protection, especially if fishing when you may not be moving about much.

Kayaking wetsuits need to allow unrestricted arm and shoulder movement. Long sleeved wetsuits are often restrictive. Avoid rear zipped wetsuits that are designed for surfing and have a neoprene collar. These are cut for surfers who spend a lot of time lying on the surfboard. The rear zip and collar when seated on a kayak is often uncomfortable, especially around the neck.

Fleeces and thermals

Fleeces are popular because they provide a lot of comfort and warmth. They are great when used by paddlers who expect to stay dry. The downside is that if you are in the water for a long time, they offer little insulation against the cold.

Combined with a wetsuit, thermals or fleece style clothing can trap extra warmth on a cooler day. It is easy to add a fleece as an extra item of clothing. Fibre pile suits can also be comfortable providing you use outer windproof shell clothing.

Shorts, vests and bathing suits

Shorts, vests and bathing suits are ideal for warm sunny days on the beach when you will never be far from the shore. Take some spare warm clothing with you to the beach as it can be hard to warm up again once you are cold. Apply high factor sun cream of SPF 30 on your exposed skin.

Outer layer or shell clothing

Paddle jackets (or cagoules) designed for kayaking give excellent protection. They are often more waterproof than other shell clothing designed for use on land and are cut for kayak activities. A simple windproof walking jacket will also work but will not be cut with kayaking in mind (closer fitting cuffs, waist and neck).

Over-trousers give extra protection on cooler days or when you are not paddling about much.

Protection for hands and feet

Paddle gloves based on those used for rowing are good options for anyone whose hands suffer from blisters or who finds they get cold quickly. Modern ultra thin neoprene gloves give good grip without the loss of sensation when holding a paddle shaft.

Footwear is important to keep your feet warm whilst paddling and when walking on the shore or on rocks. Old trainers or sandals will protect the feet. Add a pair of socks and they will keep your toes warmish.

Check your footwear will stay on if you fall in. Wellington boots should be avoided. They will end up holding lots of cold water because of their loose fit and are extremely hard to swim in. Ashore they give little ankle support.

If you wear open sandals, remember to apply sun cream to the exposed skin of your feet as the sun's rays shine directly onto this area of skin which burns easily.

Head protection is essential when messing about near solid objects. Hats keep your head warm and give sun protection. Neoprene straps can be used to keep sunglasses in place if you fall in.

Hats and helmets

Hats provide extra protection by reducing the loss of heat from the head. Neoprene caps designed for cold water make a tremendous difference afloat and are a handy item of spare kit to carry on cooler days. Putting on or taking off a hat or cap will make a big difference to how warm you feel. When fishing this is an easy way to regulate your temperature after you have reached your fishing spot and have stopped paddling.

In the surf and conditions where there is any risk of hitting solid objects such as overhanging branches or rocks you should put on a helmet.

Flotation

Below – A simple foam life jacket with leg loops and chest fastening. The leg loops are often found on jackets for young children.

Flotation aids are the most important item of safety gear to wear afloat. They come in a range of styles but with one basic aim – to keep you afloat. When choosing between them it is important to recognise the difference between buoyancy aids and life jackets. Both are sometimes called Personal Flotation Devices (PFDs).

Life jackets are designed to keep your head above water even if unconscious. They normally have a large collar around the back of the neck and most of their buoyancy toward the front and chest. Some are inflatable or partially inflatable.

Self-inflating life jackets are popular amongst boat users because they are small and lightweight. The problem is that kayaking puts us close to the water so that it is likely the device will inflate at the wrong moment! Little benefit is gained by the kayaker from an un-inflated life jacket – unless you paddle with the life jacket inflated it is not much better than a small windbreak on your body.

Buoyancy aids are designed to give inherent flotation with ease of movement. They have a balanced distribution of foam front and back (so you will be able to float on your front too).

Kayakers usually choose buoyancy aids because they give flotation, insulation and protection at all times without impeding your ability to swim. Some designs include pockets. Care needs to be exercised to avoid filling the pockets with items that will weigh the buoyancy aid down.

Simple buoyancy aid with front zip and side adjustment straps.

Ensure that your buoyancy aid is the correct size for your weight. The weight range will be printed inside the buoyancy aid. In Europe fifty Newtons (50N) of flotation is the minimum standard. In the USA standards are set by the Coastguard.

Many buoyancy aids designed for kayaking are highly adjustable to ensure a good fit. This is a good feature to consider if you expect people of different builds will be using your kayak and equipment.

A buoyancy aid with low profile pockets.

The foam flotation in a buoyancy aid degrades over time, so it is a good idea to periodically check the flotation of an old vest by weighting it down in shallow water (it should support at least 5kg). Avoid second-hand buoyancy aids unless you know their age and how well they have been looked after.

Avoid carrying too much weight in your buoyancy aid. I recall checking one paddler's buoyancy aid to find they had so much safety kit in the pockets that it sank.

KAYAKING WITH CHILDREN

*Children need correctly
sized kit to stay warm
and enjoy kayaking.*

Children need clothing and equipment that is the correct size and comfortable. On a **tandem** (two person) kayak they may not be paddling as much as an adult and are more likely to get cold.

A supply of snacks and refreshments is a great way to keep children happy as their energy levels can suddenly drop. Young children are often sitting about on a kayak paddling only a little and can easily lose interest on long trips. Build in frequent stops with young children to go ashore, explore, visit the toilet and have snacks. Most importantly you need to 'think child' and make your paddle suit the child's needs. That way they will have a great time.

Sun protection is vital for young people. Exposed skin should have high factor sun cream applied even on overcast days.

*(Opposite) Head protection is
important for young people.*

Young people love to get wet and to mess about both on the kayaks and in the water. Ensure they wear head protection, as a child's head is disproportionately heavy for their overall size.

GETTING AFLOAT

You've got all your gear together, and chosen a great little beach from which to launch. Here's how to get your kayak off the car and into the water, and look like you mean it!

Warm up

Make time for a gentle warm-up activity before starting to load or unload the kayak. Running on the spot and gentle stretching movements increase your heartbeat and warm you up and can make all the difference in avoiding injuries. On cold days take more time to warm up.

Lifting and carrying

Trolleys come in many designs. Some can be taken apart to store in a kayak hatch. It is also possible to build your own.

Most paddling related back injuries happen when lifting kayaks. Avoid carrying whenever possible – use a trolley. Dragging is also a good way to move kayaks and reduce the risk of injury. Dragging your sit-on-top over rocks, sand or concrete does wear out the bottom of the craft.

Use a trolley or buddy up to carry your kayak. Take the time to lift in a safe manner.

If you must lift a kayak then ensure you lift with good technique.

- Buddy up – there is nothing gained by lifting on your own.

- Lighten the load (make several trips if necessary).

- Use the toggles or carry handles, as strong lifting points.

- Stand with your feet shoulder width apart, keep a straight back and bend at the knees.

- Use your legs rather than your back to do the work.

- Ensure your way is clear of obstacles before you begin.

⚠ TAKE EVEN GREATER CARE WHEN LIFTING ANYTHING ABOVE CHEST HEIGHT.

Launching

From a bank or wall

A calm spot on a low sea wall, jetty, or river bank, can provide a dry way to launch your kayak.

- Sit on the bank with your kayak next to you and your bottom in line with the seat. Keep you paddle where you can reach it.

- Slide your legs into the kayak holding onto the kayak with one hand and the bank with the other.

- Keeping hold of the bank lower yourself into the seat. The movement needs to be a smooth action to avoid the kayak moving away and you taking a dip.

- Make sure you are comfortable before pushing away from the bank.

On a steeper beach this will be more difficult. On a shallower beach you will have to wade out further to float the boat.

From a beach

People often make the mistake of trying to launch the kayak while it is sitting on the beach (and have a hard time getting off the beach). It is far better to get the kayak completely afloat in knee deep water and then climb aboard. Make sure that when you climb on board, the stern of the kayak is not resting on the beach. If this does happen the kayak will rock from side to side easily on the stern which will make the kayak feel very unstable.

Getting the kayak afloat in shallow water. Slide your bottom onto the kayak seat and then swing your legs in.

In a tandem kayak, ensure the craft is afloat and put the front paddler on first. If one of the crew on a tandem is less mobile or quite young, they should be helped on board first. Ensure the tandem is in deep enough water for when the rear paddler climbs aboard.

Getting to know your kayak

Watch a young person with their first kayak and it will not be long before it is being used as diving platform, climbing frame and swimming float. It may appear to be just messing about but they are also learning what can be done with the kayak and also its limits. It's a great way to learn and improve your confidence and balance, and show off to your friends. You might even discover some new uses for your kayak. Just choose a nice calm day and plan to get very wet. This will give you a good feel for the kayak and make you less likely to fall in later!

Practising your balance and movement skills afloat will enhance your confidence levels.

PADDLE SKILLS

Grab the opportunity to sign up for sit-on-top kayak courses. Tuition will help you progress and iron out faults before they become habits. What took me years to learn by trial and error can be taught within months.

It is easy to get going without paying much attention to paddle skills. But time spent practising pays big dividends. A good range of skills will increase your confidence and encourage you to explore and discover even more from your kayak. Good skills will reduce the risk of getting into difficulty or of capsize.

This introduction is not exhaustive and there are plenty of good instructional books available which will take you further.

Forward paddling

Good forward paddling technique enables you to paddle further in comfort. Good posture and seating position is vital to ensure you get the maximum efficiency from your forward paddling. Make sure you are sitting up straight and leaning slightly forward.

- Place the paddle near the toes for maximum reach.

- The feet, hip and trunk are all working as the kayak is pulled through the water. This brings into play not just the arm muscles but the trunk and leg muscles as pressure is transferred from the foot to the tip of your fingers. If your buttocks are not moving then you are not using the lower muscles efficiently.

- Slide the kayak past the paddle. The open upper hand gives more reach and relaxes the hand.

- The blade remains near to the side of the kayak during the forward stroke and the body rotates towards the blade.

- The upper arm is pushed forward around shoulder height. The lower arm is pulling.

- The whole stroke is applied in front of the hip and body. At the hip lift the blade out of the water to commence the entry on the opposite side.

 I often visualise this action in slow motion as trying to pull the kayak through syrup.

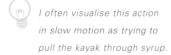 *Sometimes I trail the paddle past the hip to give a bit of steering or stability in choppy water*

There is no need to grip tightly with the top hand, as this is pushing forward. Loosen your grip and relax your hand.
The paddler's right leg is pushing against the footrest.

Push against the footrest on the same side as the active paddle. The rhythm of the feet can feel like a pedalling action.

Forward paddling on a tandem kayak

To avoid the paddles hitting each other practise paddling in time together. Learning to paddle in time increases efficiency and speed. The paddle rate is often set by the front paddler. Some larger tandem kayaks have seating positions far enough apart so as to reduce the need to paddle in time. This is useful if paddling with novices or young children.

The stronger or more experienced paddler normally paddles in the rear seat. They can control the kayak's direction and adjust their paddle rate to stay in time with the front paddler.

Paddling in strong winds

It is not just on rough days that this skill is needed. Headlands and valleys can often create localised and unexpected wind funnels.

If faced with a headwind lean forward (like cycling into the wind on a bicycle). This reduces your wind resistance and keeps your paddle stroke low. It reduces the degree to which the paddle blade will be caught by the wind. Keep a good grip on your paddle. Consider using a paddle leash in gusty conditions.

Reduce your body profile when paddling in windy conditions. Counteract the turning effect of strong winds by paddling with the blade off centre.

Turning and sweep strokes

The most common paddle technique to turn a kayak is the **sweep stroke**. Turning is achieved by sweeping your paddle in an arc away from the side of the kayak from the front to the back.

It helps to apply more foot pressure to the footrest on the same side as the stroke. Also, tilt the top edge of the paddle toward the direction of travel. This gives you a bit of support during the stroke.

● The paddle is placed to the front of the kayak with a straightened arm. Note the slight lean to assist the turn.

● The paddle is swept in an arc toward the stern. The body is turned as well.

In a tandem kayak, time your sweep strokes together to turn more effectively.

Using only part of a sweep stroke

Paddlers rarely use the whole arc of a sweep stroke. The arc can be broken down into thirds, each with slightly different effects on the kayak The middle third is most effective for turning when the boat is stopped.

The front third, good for starting a turn while on the move.

The middle third, highly effective when the boat is stationary.

Back third, easily put in at the end of a paddle stroke to correct direction.

On the move – the front third of the sweep is best for starting a turn. The back third is best for correcting course.

Paddling in a straight line

When you are trying to paddle in a straight line, as soon as the boat starts to veer off course, do a little sweep stroke using only the back third of the arc. It will stop the back of the kayak skidding and pull the stern back on line. This is sometimes called a 'correction stroke'. You can also 'push' the stern back into line using a **reverse sweep** in the last third of the arc. See also 'Stern Rudders page 43'.

Extended paddle sweeps

Sliding the hands off centre will give you a longer lever.

Sometimes sweep strokes just do not seem to be powerful enough. Perhaps the wind is coming from the side and constantly turning your kayak. A slight lean to the side the wind is coming from often reduces the problem. If this does not work, or it is uncomfortable, then extend the reach of the paddle by sliding your hand to the end of the paddle shaft. This increases the leverage of the paddle during the sweep stroke.

Reverse sweep

The reverse sweep is useful for correcting your course when paddling forward (see page 38) or combining with a foward sweep to turn 360° (see page 40).

As you might imagine, this is the sweep stroke done in reverse. Place the paddle close to the kayak behind you (you will need to rotate your body and shoulders to do this). Push the back of the paddle blade in an arc to the front of the kayak.

A slight lean to the same side as the paddle will assist the turn. If you slightly flatten the blade so the upper edge is pushed forward you will get some support for your lean.

Making a 360° turn

One paddler makes a forward sweep while the other makes a reverse sweep. Both paddlers have their bodies rotated with the stroke to get maximum efficiency.

Combine the forward sweep on the bow and the reverse sweep at the stern on the other side and you will be able to turn the kayak very quickly.

This technique works well on both tandem and single kayaks. In a single kayak you simply alternate forward and reverse sweep strokes. Just remember to rotate your body all the way before beginning the next stroke.

Stopping

If we want to avoid crashing into things we need be able to stop. Make a stopping action with a firm downward and forward push of the paddle into the water (rather like paddling backwards). Applying stopping strokes on either side to keep the kayak pointing ahead.

Aim to keep the kayak pointing in the same direction throughout and to have stopped within four reverse strokes.

Reversing

There will always be times when you cannot turn your kayak around easily, for instance when you have gone down a narrow channel to explore a cave, or need to quickly pick up something that has dropped in the water.

Paddle on each side putting the paddle blade in the water behind your hip and driving forwards. There should be some movement of the hips and an increased pressure on the ball of the foot against the footrest to use all your body during the stroke.

Turn around method

While backward paddling works well over short distances it is tedious if you need to paddle backwards out of a long narrow channel or cave. Instead swivel around on your kayak seat and paddle forwards! This is when the time spent just having fun messing about on and off your kayak starts to pay off.

If the kayak is not too wide, you can increase stability by hanging your legs over either side.

Nigel's body weight has been shifted over his left hip while he remains sitting upright with his centre of gravity central. The kayak is tilted to the left and will turn to his right.

Edging turns

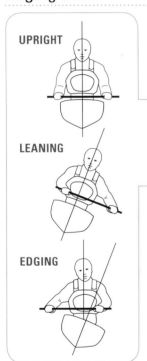

UPRIGHT

LEANING

EDGING

If the turn does not happen – experiment with the amount of tilt. Finding the exact edging point varies from kayak to kayak. If you use a wide sit-on-top, try moving your whole body slightly off centre to increase the effect.

One of the little secrets of kayaking, which enables you to subtly steer without correcting strokes. Edging is an extremely useful skill to make all your strokes and techniques work harder for you.

Edging vs leaning – when you **lean** your kayak over, your body moves too, into this potentially unstable position. When you **edge** your kayak, the boat is tilted at your hips but the aim is to keep your body upright and centred over the boat.

To make an edged turn you will continue to paddle forward as normal, but using your hips, tilt the kayak to one side.

● Paddle forward as normal.

● Transfer your weight onto your left buttock and tilt your hips.

● Your body remains upright and centred over the middle of the kayak.

● As the underwater profile of the kayak's hull changes, the kayak will turn to the right, away from the side you have edged/tilted the kayak.

When edging, some weight is transferred to the side, and you will have to use your body to balance. Time messing about in your kayak will help you to feel more confident and be able to tilt the kayak further over.

Stern rudders

You can apply quick stern rudders at the end of a forward paddling stroke by letting the paddle trail to the stern for a moment after the forward stroke.

As its name implies the paddle is held at the stern to act as a rudder, which only works while you have forward speed. You could think of it as a small reverse sweep stroke begun at the stern.

Push the paddle away from the side of the kayak as you move along. The kayak will turn in the same direction that the paddle is working (so if you place your stern rudder to your right, the kayak will turn to the right).

FOR A BETTER STERN RUDDER, ANGLE THE UPPER OR LOWER EDGE OF THE PADDLE BLADE EITHER TOWARD OR AWAY FROM THE KAYAK.

- With the paddle underwater, tilt the upper edge of the paddle away from you. This will increase the effect of the rudder and you will have to push to resist it. This will turn the kayak towards the paddle.

- Tilting the upper edge of the paddle towards you will begin to drag the paddle away from the boat and you will have to pull to resist it. This will turn the kayak away from the paddle.

Tandem stern rudders

The front paddler can continue to paddle normally while the stern rudder is made at the rear. The paddle is placed well to the back of the kayak.

Moving sideways

When paddling sideways – let go of your paddle if you feel you are going to fall in.

There will always be times when you need to move your kayak sideways; to avoid a rock, or to come alongside the bank.

Paddling sideways

Turning your whole body side-on can be a quick and simple way to move the kayak sideways. This is when the time spent messing about on the kayak will have given you confidence and when you will have learned just where your kayak's tipping point is.

Draw stroke

A more versatile method of moving sideways, the draw stroke can be quickly combined with other paddle stokes. You do not have to move your sitting position and you should keep both hands in the normal paddling grip, there is no need to change hand positions.

In tandems, draw strokes performed on opposite sides by the front and back paddlers, create a powerful 360° turn.

- Place the paddle deep in the water away from the kayak. Turn your head to look at the paddle.

- Pull the blade in to the side of the kayak, keeping the paddle shaft near vertical (your top hand will have to be near the top of your head throughout).

- Once you are happy with this sideways pulling action you can practise keeping the blade in the water and repeating the stroke.

- Having pulled the paddle to the side of the kayak, turn the paddle blade 90° and slice the paddle back out before turning it back toward you and repeating the draw stroke.

Support strokes

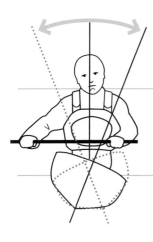

Low brace

A bracing stroke with the paddle and a flick of the hips will help to stop you falling in if knocked sideways by waves, or you lose your balance.

A hip flick is applied by transferring body weight from one hip to the other. You can practise this by wiggling your hips; stay sitting upright and rock the boat over from one edge to the other. Try to make the movement strong and snappy.

Low brace – the back of the paddle blade is pressed onto the surface of the water and a hip flick is applied to stop you going over.

The spine on the back of the paddle should be downward as you press on the water. It is the hip flick, not the push down on the paddle, which does the work of keeping you upright.

High brace

The low brace is a stable and comfortable position, however, sometimes you may need to recover from further off balance, this is when the high brace is useful.

⚠ *Avoid lifting the paddle too high during the high brace as it can lead to shoulder injuries. Keeping your elbows bent will allow them to act as shock absorbers.*

The drive face of the paddle should be downward as you press on the water. Your wrists and elbows hang under the paddle shaft. The high brace can be used to recover from a greater angle but places much more strain on your body – for that reason the low brace should be your first line of defence.

Low brace turn

A low brace turn sequence. Sweep on the left; low brace and lean to the right; paddle away.

The low brace turn is a very efficient way to turn while moving which gives you some support as you lean into the turn.

The turn is started by a forward sweep stroke then, on the opposite side, the back of the paddle blade is placed on the surface of the water well out to the side and just behind your hip.

Lean into the turn and push back upright to paddle away when you have completed your turn.

RESCUES

People often ask what happens if they fall in. My reply is pretty simple "You get wet". It is one of the big worries for novice kayakers. But in a sit-on-top there is no need to extract your legs from a cockpit or any need to remove a spray deck before you can bail out, instead you'll simply fall off into the water. Then you can clamber back on top.

Practise swimming and rescues from your kayak so you know what to do when it happens for real. This will reduce any fears of dealing with a capsize and increase your confidence. Practice will also alert you to any potential problems you may encounter with your kit or technique before you really need to do a real rescue.

Self rescue (fast method)

The quickest method (which requires a degree of athleticism).

- Immediately after capsizing make sure you have hold of the paddle and kayak to stop them drifting away.

- Flip the kayak over. A paddle leash can reduce the risk of the paddle drifting away.

- Reach for the opposite side and pull yourself onto the kayak. Kick your legs.

- Swivel the body upright. Swing your legs into the kayak in a smooth action as your centre of gravity is quite high.

This method requires balance and agility to swing your legs in. Try it out when messing around, after all, if you fall in, you're already wet!

Lying along the boat when bringing your legs on board keeps your centre of gravity low to help your balance. Straddling the kayak with your legs in the water as you sit up also helps with balance.

Self rescue (stable method)

This method is similar to the previous rescue except it involves keeping the body lying horizontal across the kayak for as long as possible. The legs are used to give extra stability at the moment you move to sit upright.

- The body is now swung horizontal to the kayak with the legs hanging over either side. The centre of gravity remains low.

- Both legs are in the water to give stability before swinging the body upright and onto the seat.

This works especially well for the larger or less mobile paddler.

⚠ BULKY BUOYANCY AIDS CAN MAKE GETTING BACK ON BOARD DIFFICULT SO AVOID CARRYING LOTS OF KIT IN YOUR POCKETS. DO NOT REMOVE YOUR BUOYANCY AID WHEN TRYING TO CLIMB BACK ON BOARD YOUR KAYAK.

Over stern method

Kicking down with your legs in the water will help you pull yourself onto the kayak's stern. The over stern method can be difficult if you have equipment stored on the rear deck or if your kayak has a raised and solid back rest.

Crawl up the stern of the kayak keeping your legs spread apart and your head and chest low.

Tandem rescue

If you can hang your legs over the sides you will make the kayak more stable.

The key is to use one of the crew to act as the counter balance as the other paddler gets back on board. Be prepared to help pull each other back on board and keep your centre of gravity low (keep your head and chest ducked down toward the boat).

Assisted rescue

If there's a second kayaker to help hold your kayak and to pull you in, this will speed up the rescue. Have them lie low across your deck and grip your bow under their armpit.

COMMUNICATION BETWEEN BOTH PADDLERS WILL SPEED UP THE RESCUE – SO TALK TO EACH OTHER. ALWAYS WAIT UNTIL ALL THE PADDLERS HAVE SORTED THEMSELVES OUT BEFORE LETTING GO OF THE KAYAK.

Baling out

Occasionally the inside chamber of the kayak may become filled with water if a drain bung is not properly in place or a storage hatch is leaking.

If the hull starts to fill with water the best option is to get to shore to sort out the problem. If this is not possible the kayak needs to be pulled across another kayak and turned upside down to drain the water away out of the hatch or drain hole.

When the swamped kayak is pulled up onto the deck of the rescuer's kayak, the X shape formed by the two makes a very stable platform and allows repairs to be carried out. In choppy water a paddler may need to remain in the water while repairing or emptying the kayak.

An alternative option is to consider towing the filling kayak while the kayaker sits or lies on your kayak as you head for shore (see Towlines, page 57).

An 'X' rescue can be used make a repair afloat.

IF THE REPAIR TAKES LONGER THAN EXPECTED LOOK OUT FOR HYPOTHERMIA. MAKE SURE THE PERSON IN THE WATER KEEPS HOLD OF THE KAYAK AS YOU MAY OTHERWISE DRIFT AWAY FROM THEM.

Ensure your self-rescue and paddle skills are well practised in all conditions. Practising a self-rescue on a calm sunny day is of minimal value if you have never tested the technique in rougher water. Practise where conditions are testing but consequences are not serious. Then if the paddler is unable to self-rescue the wind will push him into the calmer water of the nearby sheltered bay.

STAYING SAFE

Preparation and practice as well as knowledge of the environment you are paddling in will increase your safety margin. You may not be able to prevent an accident, but the right equipment, skills or know-how may turn a potential crisis into an adventure.

Paddling as a group

Paddling with others is an opportunity to watch your friends catching the big fish, discovering the depths of a cave or neatly nipping between a rocky gully before a swell crashes behind them.

Two is company, but three offers more security. If you encounter a problem you have someone with you who can provide assistance and someone who can go for help if necessary.

When paddling with others ensure that you all know:

- The route.

- Who is in the group.

- What safety kit is carried.

- That the trip is within your level of ability.

Trip organisers do make mistakes or forget things so be prepared to ask questions or raise doubts. It is better to ask who has the tow-line at the start than to discover it has been forgotten when you need it.

Voice your concerns if you think things are not going right. Often others will be feeling the same. If you are paddling with people you do not know, then check their plans to ensure that you are going to be paddling within your comfort zone.

It is better to cancel or change a planned paddle than to slog on and have a calamity. Coastlines, islands and great locations will still be there tomorrow if you decide to cancel.

A group is only as strong as the weakest member. If you find you are paddling with people who do not recognise this then it is time to find others to paddle with.

Solo paddling

Paddling solo is more risky. The margins for error are reduced and it is easy for relatively minor mishaps to escalate quickly. Retrieving a dropped paddle on a windy day can soon become a major mishap. When things start to go wrong you are on your own. Even on a busy beach, by the time people realise you may be in trouble it could be too late. Just because lots of people are about does not mean that they will recognise that you may be in difficulty.

Most paddlers seriously underestimate how hard it is to right and get back on board their kayak after a capsize. Even on a tandem it is difficult without the help of another kayak. If you cannot self-rescue in the conditions you find then you must reconsider your trip.

If you do paddle alone be well prepared and know your limits. Allow yourself an extra safety margin; only venture afloat alone on calm days and in areas that you know are less remote.

Float plans

Whenever you go on the water, ensure someone is aware of your plans and knows:

If you subsequently change plans ensure your land contact is informed.

- Where you are going.

- Departure and return time.

- Who you are going with.

- Details of the craft – colour etc.

- What forms of communication you are carrying (have you checked they work?)

Your land contact should also know what action they should take and who they should inform if you do not make contact by the agreed time. Around the British coast this will normally be the Coastguard, while inland it will be the Police.

Set realistic return times and agree the time that they should call for the rescue services. It will hamper your rescue if the emergency services are not alerted until it is way past your return time and darkness is falling.

Even if you do inform the Coastguard or rescue service of your plans, they will not normally commence a search until your land support has alerted them. It is for this reason that you should ensure the land contact is well briefed and reliable.

Your safety kit

Before going afloat always check that your equipment and kayak are in good order. Always check any drain plugs are secure and have not been fiddled with by friends or small children.

Basic safety kit (left).
Additional safety kit for
going to sea (right).

The safety kit you carry will depend on the area, type of water, weather conditions and your level of competence. There is no point in carrying safety equipment you do not know how to use. Most importantly, keep it simple.

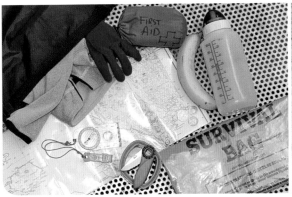

If you fish from the kayak, carry a pair of wire snips capable of cutting hooks which might become embedded in your hand.

I also include a clean kitchen J Cloth. This can be used to dry your hands before opening first aid packs, or using mobile phones.

A notepad and pencil are useful for calculating your course, and also for recording details during medical emergencies.

Though rarely seen in Britain, a small signal mirror for reflecting the sun can also be a great way to attract attention.

A basic safety kit might consist of:

- Adequate clothing for the conditions.

- Small first aid pack to cover minor cuts and bumps.

- A roll of tape to make repairs to the kayak or equipment.

- A compass and map if you are paddling in an unfamiliar area or where there is a risk of poor visibility.

- Whistle to attract attention, which should be attached to your buoyancy aid.

- Knife. This does not have to be the size of a machete. It just needs to be capable of cutting tangled cord etc.

- A snack to eat and drink but avoid alcohol.

- Money for phone calls or cups of tea.

- A survival bag (one of those thick orange plastic sacks).

Keep all this in a small waterproof grab bag clearly marked with the contents. For added waterproofing, package groups of items separately in transparent freezer bags.

Communication afloat

Mobile phones (cell phones)

Mobile phones are often useful providing you recognise that there are still many areas where coverage is limited or non-existent. Many of the best kayaking areas on rivers or sea are out of range.

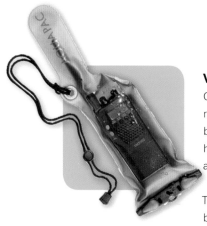

VHF radios

On the sea the Coastguard recommend the use of VHF marine radio hand held transceivers (not to be confused with Citizen's band radios) because anyone listening on the safety channel will hear you. Calls are free and you can receive weather forecasts and inform the Coastguard of any delays or changes of plan.

A VHF radio allows you to talk to anyone who is listening – a mobile phone only allows the person called to hear you.

Though VHF marine hand held units require a licence they can be bought over the counter at reasonable cost and are often waterproof or splash resistant. Classes and study aids will enable you to pass a simple user test. Contact your local adult education centre or sailing club to find out when courses are being run to teach good radio communication.

Flares

At sea and on large lakes flares are recommended. There are many different types, not all makes are waterproof. They have a limited shelf life and must be replaced periodically.

For most coastal trips I carry two hand held smoke flares and a red flare. These are packed in waterproof bags or home-made flare tubes.

Smoke flares emit a large cloud of bright orange smoke to grab attention in daylight. **Red flares** produce an intense flame which is like a Roman candle firework. It is designed for use at night or in poor visibility. Though you may not plan to be out in the dark or poor visibility this is when many incidents occur. By the time your shore support has alerted the rescue services of your late return it may well be approaching nightfall and a red flare is therefore very useful. Small **mini flare units** are useful to pinpoint your location once an alert is called. Mini flares have many cartridges to fire off and are easy to carry but are not always easy to see.

White flares are also available and are used to alert vessels of your presence.

If each paddler in a group has just one flare then you have a lot of smoke/flares to signal an emergency. The shortcoming of flares is that they do rely upon someone seeing them and recognising that they are a distress signal and not just a pretty plume of smoke.

Hand-held smoke, flare, rocket and pinpoint mini flares with waterproof bag and home-made flare tube (with plastic cleat attached to the lid to aid opening and securing).

Home-made flare tubes made from plastic drainpipe components can produce a waterproof and sturdy flare container.

 Distress flares are powerful pyrotechnic devices. They must be stored and disposed of safely. Learn how flares work. Many yacht clubs organise annual flare demonstrations.

Towlines

The paddler being towed is still able to paddle, he is being helped rather than rescued.

This is probably the most useful item of rescue kit you can carry at sea. I describe a towline as a helping hand for when a member of the group is finding paddling a bit hard. Rather than wait until a person is completely exhausted, you should commence the tow while they can continue to paddle. This is less tiring for the person towing and less demoralising for the person on tow.

Whether you select a boat or body attached towline ensure it can be released and attached quickly.

Many towlines have a built in length of shock cord which absorbs the shock when the line suddenly becomes taut. In the absence of a towline any length of cord or webbing will suffice, but always ensure that you can easily release the tow.

⚠ Avoid towing in surf or on a river. On a river it may be better to help a swimmer to shore then get the boat. In the surf it is better to get the person to swim in to shore holding onto their kayak while you stay well clear. This reduces the risk of people being hit by the kayaks or entangled in the towline.

WEATHER AND THE KAYAKER

Whenever you plan to go afloat it is vital to check the weather forecast. The best forecasts are those for specific areas and issued close to the time you want to go paddling. Long-range forecasts will give a good indication of likely trends to help you plan your trip even a week in advance. However, you must be prepared to change your plans on the day.

Wind

Beware wind that may be blowing offshore (on the sea, lakes or large rivers). This can make your return to shore harder as you will be paddling into the wind. The great danger of offshore winds is that if you are unable to cope you will be blown further out. Onshore winds can make for safer paddling as they return you to shore if you stop paddling.

A following wind (blowing from behind you) will whiz you along but result in a hard paddle back against the wind. Take a moment to turn around and paddle back toward your start point just to get an idea of how strong the wind might be on your return. It also means you can more easily remember what your launching point looks like from the water.

Winds of above Beaufort force 3 (7-10 mph) will be hard work to paddle against and you may start getting problems steering your kayak. Until you have got used to paddling in winds, stick to going afloat when the wind is below force 3 or select locations where landing is easy and there is little risk of being blown offshore.

Even a light headwind can make forward paddling hard work. Note the small ripples on the surface. The wind shown in this photo turned a great paddle into a bit of a slog on our return.

It is possible to paddle when there are stronger winds by selecting areas that are protected from the wind. Often this is beneath cliffs, in bays and behind islands, where you will be sheltered. Be very careful not to venture out of the sheltered areas or you will lose the protection provided by the land. You can spot where this is happening by looking for the ripples and waves on the water. It is best to get practice by going on training courses or out with experienced kayakers.

Calm conditions close beneath cliffs while an offshore force 4 was blowing. Note the darker stripe of ripples behind the paddlers. A kayak group paddling 300 yards away had a paddler capsized by the gusting wind.

On lakes and large rivers as well as the sea you can also encounter unexpected strong winds and gusts even on otherwise calm days as cooling air is funnelled down valleys or forced over hilltops.

Take time to check the weather forecasts and to note if the wind direction is going to change while you are on the water. Even a small change of direction can make a sheltered cove become more difficult to launch from after a day spent picnicking on the beach. A change of wind direction can also make a headland or point more difficult to round even if the wind strength may not have increased.

Sun

SLIP ON A TOP.
SLAP ON A HAT.
SLOP ON YOUR
SUN BLOCK.

The water reflects sunlight and harmful UV rays. Everybody should take steps to avoid sunburn, and wear sunglasses on bright days.

High factor sun block cream is recommended and UV protective clothing is now available. You can still burn through a T-shirt or fleece style top even in British waters. Take some liquids afloat (not alcohol) to avoid dehydration, which can occur even on a warm overcast day. Children, in particular, need protection from the sun's effects.

SEA AND SURF

When on the sea it is important to remember that even though you may be paddling in a tiny sheltered bay, you are connected to and affected by a vast body of water.

The beach is an excellent place to enjoy using your sit-on-top. Popular bathing beaches often attract small surf which is an excellent place to play and to develop new skills.

The surf zone

Whether you need to land or want to do a spot of surfing, keep clear of other beach users. Avoid landing in the safe swimming areas that are marked on many beaches.

After a great trip there is nothing worse than to arrive back at a busy beach loaded with fishing gear and a great catch and to then experience the embarrassment of a capsize as you land through the surf. Your pride takes a tumble as you emerge wet and sand-covered in front of the family. You also risk damaging kit, yourself and others as the kayak is flung onto the beach. An out of control kayak can be likened to a tree trunk. Anyone in its path is going to get hurt. If you find yourself in this situation, stay clear and avoid getting caught between the incoming kayak and the shore.

Never underestimate the power of even small waves. Practise in small surf well clear of other users. Secure and stow away loose kit and make sure any leashes or attachments will not become entangled with you.

Rip currents may pull continuously or may suddenly appear or intensify. Rip currents can aid your departure through the surf but also can sweep swimmers out into deep water.

Generally, the more open a bay is to ocean swells then the more likely it is that you will get surf. Beaches that are very flat may be prone to large surf. The presence of surfers is a good indication that the beach is a surf beach. The sides of the bay frequently have smaller surf, as do areas where the currents run out of the bay. If there are strong **rip currents** then landing may be hard. Rips are often a sign of beaches that get a lot of surf.

Rip currents

As waves spill onto the beach water is piling up there and has to flow away. It will sometimes do this around the sides of the bay or by a rivermouth. These currents away from the beach are called rips and are not always obvious to spot.

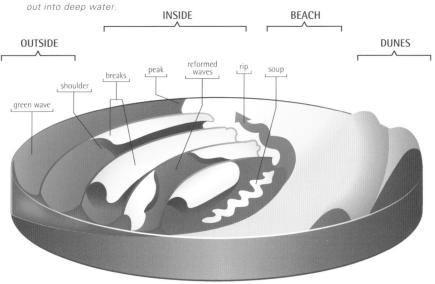

This effect may be caused by a rising tide. Conversely, a falling tide can lead to surf decreasing.

On some beaches, strong offshore currents across the mouth of a bay can block out the waves. Only as the current decreases will the waves be able to reach the beach and create larger surf. This is sometimes the reason why surf can intensify quickly.

Landing and launching in the surf

Landing through surf can be fun or a pain. A lot depends upon whether you want to ride the waves or not. If not, consider whether the beach you launch from may have surf when you return. As you look at the launch site you will spot places where the surf is likely to be smaller. If the bay is used by board surfers then check with them where the surf is usually smaller.

Controlled landing

Rather than ride in with the wave pushing you from behind the aim is to land just behind the wave as it surges up the beach. This keeps you in control.

If you find the next wave rearing up behind you, paddle hard backwards. Once you are over the wave try to stay just behind it as it surges up the beach.

Grab and drag other kayakers higher up the beach where they will be able to step off without being buffetted by the waves.

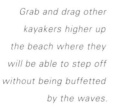

Surfed landing on a low brace

Expect to get wet and wear a helmet if you have one. Shorter kayaks will be easier to control while surfing than longer kayaks.

● The low support is ready just before the wave hits.

● The paddle is placed onto the top of the wave crest while you lean toward the paddle.

● When hit by a wave lean toward the wave to avoid a capsize.

● You will slide/bounce sideways on the wave toward the shore (sometimes called a 'bongo slide').

Just leaving the blade
horizontal on the surface
of the water will provide support in
case a wave catches you unaware.

Surfing it up

For a dynamic surfed landing use a stern rudder on either side to keep your bow pointing toward the shore. As the wave breaks, expect to be turned sideways and be ready with your brace.

- As the wave builds behind you start to paddle forward.

- Once on the wave use the stern rudder to steer.

- As the kayak starts to turn side on to the wave lean toward the wave and brace.

Dumping surf

Some beaches have an obvious steep slope. This indicates that the beach is liable to experience heavy breaking surf that rears up and crashes onto the beach. Given the chance it will grind you into the beach. Worse still there will often be a strong pull back by the wave (an undertow) as it recedes from the beach before the arrival of the next wave. This will pull the legs from under anyone trying to stand up or scramble up the beach.

If you need to land or launch in dumping surf ensure all kit is stowed away, and land following just behind the wave as it advances up the beach, paddle fast to drive your kayak as far up the beach as possible. Be ready to jump off quickly and grab the kayak before the wave starts to recede. Otherwise you and your kayak will be pulled back into the next wall of water.

Paddling out through surf

If you can find an easy place to launch then use it. Surf can be powerful and gear can easily be washed away. Remember that the surf may be bigger on your return.

Surf waves come in sets. You might typically get two or three small waves, followed by two or three medium waves, followed by two or three larger waves, then the cycle repeats. Sit on your kayak afloat and wait until the sets of waves seem to be smaller then make your paddle out beyond the breaking waves.

Lean forward and put the paddle into the water as the wave is about to hit the bow.

- Paddle quickly toward the oncoming waves.

- As the wave is about to hit the bow lean well forward and dig the paddle in deep.

- As soon as the wave hits your body make another deep paddle stroke on the other side, to pull you through the wave.

- Paddle fast until you are well clear of the break. You may need to vary your speed to time your way out through the breaks.

Tides and currents

Tide tables and a tidal stream atlas are vital tools to consult before going on the sea. At the very least they may save you returning to find yourself with a long trudge across an empty bay.

On any beach you need to know the times of high and low tide and also which way the currents are flowing. Off **headlands** (where the land sticks out into the sea at the edges of a bay) conditions can change dramatically when the tide starts to rise or fall.

Tidal currents can lead you into areas that are far from safe landing spots. Take time to learn about them and how the directions and speeds can change on the sea.

Currents are often stronger off headlands where you may also encounter rough water. This is a result of the increased flow of water around the headlands and their rocky reefs.

A tidal race (or overfalls) forming off of a headland as the tidal currents are squeezed around the land. Calmer water lies to either side of the headland.

Wind against tide

At sea, if the wind is blowing in the same direction as the current (wind with tide) the sea may become less rough. However, if the wind is blowing in the opposite direction to the current expect the sea to become rougher. This is known as wind against tide. This can catch out the unwary kayaker returning around a headland after the tide has turned, finding much rougher conditions.

RIVER PADDLING

On all but the slowest of rivers it is important to remember that, even when you are not paddling, you are being swept along by the current. Most of the time this is very helpful but you need to look well ahead to plan your route and avoid being swept into a dangerous situation. Spot obstructions well in advance and paddle to avoid them while you are still well upstream.

Bends

On a straight section of river the current is fastest in the middle and slowest near the banks. On a bend the fast current sets into the outside of the bend. This can sweep the unwary into overhanging branches or debris (known as strainers). Strainers can be extremely dangerous where there is a fast current as the paddler or swimmer can be trapped like a fish in a net.

The current sweeps toward the outside of the bend and the paddlers stay in midstream by paddling toward the inside of the bend in good time.

The good news is that on easy rivers these strainers are easily avoided. Simply look well ahead downstream and on approaching a bend paddle toward the inside of the bend to stay in midstream.

Drops and weirs

It is important to realise that these may turn up even on relatively calm and sluggish rivers. If you are not sure whether a drop formed by a natural rapid or a man-made weir (low head dam) is safe, you can simply get off the river upstream of it, carry your boat around the hazard and put back in downstream. This is known as a portage.

Weirs should be avoided. Even the most innocuous looking weir can result in entrapment.

IF IN DOUBT, GET OUT!

So how do we spot drops from upstream?

Rapids are usually noisy; you will probably hear the roaring of the rapid from a fair way off. Although you may not be able to see the whitewater at the bottom of the drop you may be able to see the tail end of the waves formed by the rapid further downstream. You may also see spray formed by the water pouring over the drop.

Weirs, particularly dangerous weirs, can be very quiet, with the water gurgling rather than roaring. However, the water that is held back by the weir forms a 'weir pool', so if the river has been running at a steady rate and the water suddenly becomes a calm pool, there is probably a weir just downstream.

A warning sign that occurs on both weirs and steep drops is sometimes known as an 'event horizon'. This occurs when you can see the foreground and the distant ground, but the middle ground seems to disappear.

Feet and hands near the surface. You can progress toward the bank by swimming at an angle – crossing the current at an angle of 45°.

Swimming in fast flowing water

In slow water, if you fall in, you may well have time to perform one of the self rescues described earlier (page 48). In faster flowing water you may need to swim your kayak to the side first or even save yourself and then chase your kayak down the bank.

In deep water you can swim any way you like. In shallow water or where there may be hidden obstructions swim on your back keeping your feet and hands on the surface. If a foot or hand gets caught you will be pushed to the bottom by the force of the water … and held there. It is also a good idea to keep your feet downstream to fend off any boulders that you may be swept onto.

River grades are noted in various river, canoe touring or whitewater guidebooks. Talk to local paddlers, they will often also refer to the river's grade.

Grades

Rivers are graded from class one to class six. Before venturing on any river of more than a class two it is essential that you get instruction in whitewater paddling skills, and safety and rescue techniques. Many outdoor centres run these excellent courses which will increase your skills and knowledge.

You may find information on river levels in guidebooks to the area, or by talking to local paddlers. If it has been raining persistently you can expect high levels.

Water level and flood

Rivers follow an annual cycle of high water and low water. The river may be high during rainy months (in places like Britain) or during hot spells (when the glaciers melt in the Alps). The water level will affect how fast the river flows, the water quality (more silt may be stirred up), how much debris there is floating in the rivers and how easy it is to get to the banks. It is safest to paddle at low or medium levels.

⚠ FLOOD WARNING! WHEN THE RIVER HAS BURST ITS BANKS IT IS IN FLOOD. THIS MAY HAPPEN AFTER SPORADIC STORMS OR HEAVY RAIN. SOMETIMES, ON DAMMED RIVERS, THERE MAY BE UNSCHEDULED RELEASES OF WATER. DO NOT PADDLE WHEN THE RIVER IS IN FLOOD.

DIVING AND SCUBA

This does mean you might find yourself diving in more remote places so ensure you have proper training.

Sit-on-tops offer great opportunities to sneak off around the coast into coves and caves that are otherwise difficult to reach by other boats. For anyone keen on snorkelling or scuba you can dive in places that few others will ever visit without an exhausting surface swim. The paddle to the dive site also acts as a good warm-up activity.

With a stable platform and the large storage area at the stern of many sit-on-tops, the carrying of diving and scuba gear is possible as many promotional photos show. However in temperate waters (such as those around the UK) it is important to consider the water temperature and follow safe diving practices. Do not dive alone. The British Sub Aqua Club (BSAC) and Professional Association of Diving Instructors (PADI) centres run lots of learn to dive courses.

Wetsuits worn for diving are thicker and more restrictive than those used for paddling so you might need to consider landing ashore to change back into your paddling gear.

If you are going to try diving from the kayak practise putting on kit and your dive routines in shallow water so that if you drop anything overboard it is easier to retrieve and problems can be

Rope or shock cord tethers attached to the kayak eyelets can be used to stop bits of diving kit getting lost while you prepare to dive.

Very experienced divers advocate hanging kit on a line over the side in the order you will need to put it on. That way it stays safe and is less likely to lead to an unplanned dip or kit being dropped or knocked over board.

easily sorted out. Practise your dives in very calm conditions until you are sure you feel confident and learn how to organise your kit close to the shore in order to build up confidence. Ensure you can climb back on board your kayak. Kit can easily get snagged while climbing aboard. You may need to practise removing any bulky or heavy kit. This is all tricky stuff.

In most cases, unless you are very experienced, it is prudent to find a spot to land at and then get ready with your dive kit. If you put kit on afloat get your flippers on quickly so they give you more stability while your feet hang over the side and other bits of dive gear are adjusted and fitted.

Having completed the dive you are likely to be feeling cold. The return paddle may well leave you feeling colder. Carry a paddle jacket. Land on a nearby beach to put on paddling clothing.

Some divers attach the kayak to themselves while diving. This poses the risk of entanglement, so carry a knife. It can also produce a lot of resistance while you swim underwater especially if the wind or currents pick up.

If you anchor the kayak the anchor line provides a useful line to descend and ascend but you do need to consider that currents may carry you away from the kayak.

If the kayak is left afloat while you dive ensure all paddle kit is secure. A lost paddle is no fun and your flippers do not make good paddles. Also, add a recognised dive marker as other water users may come over to check on an apparently abandoned kayak that appears to be drifting on the water.

See the resources section (page 87) at the back of the book for a few diving related websites that may be of interest.

Similarly if you land on a deserted or remote beach to snorkel or scuba it is worth indicating you are diving nearby as your kayak might look abandoned. Surfacing to find your kayak is being towed away could lead to a long and potentially dangerous swim back.

KAYAK FISHING

If there is one activity that has seen a huge growth with the use of sit-on-tops, it is fishing. Much can be written about how to fish which is outside the scope of this book. A web search can provide a wealth of information on 'yak fishing', fishing techniques and kit (you will find a list of some websites in the back of the book).

Kitting the kayak out

A paravane attaches on your line and keeps your lures from being dragged to the surface.

A consideration when fishing from a kayak is to decide if you are going to use a rod or hand line. Hand lines are easy to carry and can be dropped overboard or trawled along behind you as you paddle. Using a **paravane** that allows the lure to stay at a fixed depth reduces some of the problem of the lure rising to the surface as you paddle. However, it does add drag.

> ⚠ BE VERY CAREFUL IF YOU TIE FISHING LINES TO YOUR KAYAK. A 4LB BASS CAN PULL STRONGLY MAKING A HAND LINE TIED TO THE SIDE OF THE KAYAK VERY HARD TO UNTIE. IT IS HOWEVER GOOD FUN TO WATCH SOMEONE BEING PULLED SIDEWAYS BY THEIR CATCH AS THEY STRUGGLE TO UNTIE THE LINE! ALWAYS CARRY A KNIFE.

Ready to fish. Note the fish finder on the orange kayak.

Using a fishing rod is more versatile than a hand line, particularly when playing a fish, but is less compact. Telescopic fishing rods are easy to store but can be a bit flimsy.

Attaching gear to the kayak is open to debate. On the plus side you will not lose gear should the kayak tip over. The downside is that there is an increased risk of lines becoming tangled around you if you fall in.

Keep your kit simple, don't take what you won't need.

- Carry a knife on your person to cut tangled ropes or lines.

- Stow gear so that hooks and lines do not get in your way.

- When landing, avoid surf or rough water to lessen the risk of broken or lost fishing gear if it is lying on the deck.

Learning to move about and turn around on your kayak while afloat is an essential skill to master before you add the complication of fishing from your kayak. Fun time spent messing about balancing on your kayak begins to pay off, as you can move around confidently on your kayak to put gear into hatches or reach for equipment.

Staying safe

Learn about the waters you fish and how to kayak on them safely. I come across many people fishing from kayaks whose knowledge of the lakes, rivers and coastline they are paddling is very poor and who have limited kayak skills. This puts them at risk.

There is a big difference between fishing from a bank, headland or pier and being afloat on a kayak. Even if you have fished from a boat, a kayak is a different sort of craft with its own advantages and disadvantages.

 Take time to learn about the movement of water, local conditions and weather. Always keep an eye on what is happening around you.

It is easy to get carried away fishing and not notice that you are drifting offshore or around a headland. If winds are blowing offshore or away from the beach then spend a few minutes first, paddling a short distance back to shore to feel how strong the wind really is. You may be drifting out of your sheltered bay.

Being passed by a high speed ferry travelling at 35 knots, which was close enough to see the grin on the faces of the passengers, was not much fun and the wash nearly threw me in.

Check if you are likely to be near shipping lanes or areas of small craft traffic. Spotting a stationary kayak fishing is not easy from a small boat and it is easy for you not to notice or hear vessels approaching if they are down-wind of you.

Boat colour

A surprising number of kayaks are sold in drab green and camouflage colours. This is perhaps fine for river and lake fishing but at sea you are making yourself very hard to spot. At sea, orange and other bright colours increase your visibility.

Other boat users may not be expecting to see a small kayak and any waves can make you harder to spot.

When paddling, the glint of the moving paddle blades will often alert others to your presence. When stationary a small flag attached to a pole can be a good marker. Some designs of kayak include screw in fittings to allow a small pole for a small flag or even a radar reflector. This can indicate to people on the shore that the fact that you have seemed to be stationary for a long time does not mean you are in trouble.

Ensure you have a compass and know how to use it even if you are using a GPS. Try 'Sea Kayak Navigation' by Franco Ferrero for a practical manual on navigation.

Fishing in poor visibility

Early morning can be a great time to fish but you must ensure you can be seen. A small pole with an all round light is useful if you are fishing so others know you are there. Carry a torch as all craft need to be able to show a light.

Casting

There are a lot of promotional pictures about showing people standing up to cast from a kayak. Unless you have practised this a lot this is to be avoided except in water that is shallow enough to stand up in if you fall. Even some of the widest sit-on-tops are not stable enough for standing casts.

If you do fall in whilst casting you will have to deal with a surprise dunking and also avoid tangling up in your fishing rod and tackle.

It's safer to sit and cast – after all, your kayak has helped you get closer to the fish already.

Clothing for fishing

Don't overload your pockets with fishing gear – stow it in a bag or box.

A capsize while you have a jumper over your head is a very frightening experience.

Whilst fishing from a kayak, you will not only be paddling but also be spending a lot of time stationary. Fishing clothing is often unsuitable for kayaking and kayaking clothing is a better bet. Carry extra clothing and remember that it needs to be easy to put on and take off. If you need to change what you are wearing it is often far easier and safer to spend a few minutes paddling back to shore rather than trying to put clothing on while afloat.

Fishing safety gear

Eye protection and a hat are a good idea when dealing with hooks and lines.

A small pair of sharp, strong flat nose pliers should be able to cut through smaller hooks.

Give some consideration to what protective clothing and kit you will take afloat. Rusty old hooks always tend to be the ones that get yanked into your finger, so a way of cutting the shank is worth taking with you. Paddling back with an embedded hook is no fun.

Eye protection and hats are always a good idea. A snagged hook and weight that comes free suddenly might hit you in the face. A hat and sunglasses at least offer a little more protection without needing to go into protective clothing overdrive.

Once you have a catch, it's up to you whether you choose to use a net, but you do need to consider how you will keep hold of the fish and de-hook it without losing gear overboard or transferring hooks into your hands. Forceps style hook disgorgers can help keep hooks out of hands. Floating pliers and snips can be bought.

Fishing equipment

Plastic storage crates can be modified to fit onto the stern compartment.
© Scotty / Rob Jones

Storage
Fishing takes up a lot of space afloat on a kayak and the item you need always seems to be in the most inaccessible place. The more you take out the more the risk of it falling into the water.

Consider just how much kit you need to take on the water. Many people fish with a small hook/lure weight box and a bait box. Extra items can be left ashore to be collected if needed, as the more gear you carry the more risk there is of losing it in choppy water. Worse, it may inhibit your ability to paddle.

Storage pouches can be cable tied or fastened to the storage box. Small bags or even a collapsible plastic bowl can be used to store bait and other items inside a hatch if no mesh netting is in place to stop things sliding out of reach. A bit of netting over the catch box can reduce the risk of losing your catch.

 If you prefer to put the catch straight into the hatch of your kayak, remember how many fish you have caught. Finding a rotting fish inside the kayak later is not pleasant!

A simple rocket launcher style holder for mounting on the kayak.

Rod holders

It is easy to get carried away with the number of rods taken afloat. Fishing with six rods using the stern rod holder tubes and triple rocket launcher style rod holders mounted on the deck is serious fishing. You might even find the local fisheries protection team questioning whether you are in fact a commercial fisherman.

Get plenty of experience kayak fishing before using more than one rod, as the potential for tangles and problems multiplies rapidly. Unlike a dinghy, you are sitting on top of a small floating platform that reacts to your every move. Also, it is worth considering what you will do if you hit the bass shoal of the year that is just starving hungry and desperate to bite every hook you have out at the same time. Sometimes our dreams come true.

There is always a risk of dropping your rod into the water. Small lengths of shock cord attaching the reels and rod to the rod holders can reduce the likelihood of this happening. However, they need to be easy to release.

Whatever you do, always ensure that you stow all gear away before landing if it looks as if there is any risk of landing in even small surf. You should have practised moving about on your kayak before you really need to do this. It is a good reason for having spent time doing balancing and fun things with your kayak.

A fish finder mounted on the kayak with a compass mounted on the front hatch cover.

© Scotty / Rob Jones

Fish finders and satellite navigation systems

If you really start getting serious about fishing then a GPS (Global Positioning System) and fish finder are worth considering. The GPS will not only help you locate the good spots again but may also help you get home if the fog rolls in.

⚠ WITH ANY PIECE OF ELECTRONIC EQUIPMENT YOU NEED TO MAKE SURE YOU ARE PREPARED FOR THE DAY THAT IT FAILS TO WORK. BATTERIES RUN DOWN, CONTACTS CORRODE AND HOUSINGS LEAK.

I can recall a number of trips when I first had a GPS with me that I would never have attempted without one. Once I discovered that equipment can fail, I learned to not push the limits as much.

A navigation aid like GPS is precisely that: an aid. The risk is that they can lead us into pushing our limits. The technology can lull us into believing we can attempt more because we know exactly where we are.

A web search can reveal lots of information on fish finders and retro-fit fishing modifications. Just ensure that if you drill any holes to affix your fish finder, you make them in the correct place and they are well sealed to stop water entering the hull. The old saying "the only thing that is totally waterproof is a frog's ear" is worth remembering when undertaking modifications and using supposedly waterproof gear.

Anchors and sea anchors

Once you have found your favourite fishing spot it can be a pain to keep drifting away from it. If you use an anchor make sure it is small (around 0.75kg), is easy to store on board and pull in.

Small grapnel style anchors (top) and drogues (bottom) (also called sea anchors) keep you from drifting too far.

⚠ *An anchor can work well on still water but can become a dangerous if it becomes snagged and you are in a current.*

Sea anchors (sometimes called drogues or sea socks) will stop you drifting down wind. However, a sea anchor will not stop the current from pulling you along. Be aware of where you are drifting. Trying to pull in a sea anchor as you round a rough headland is not advised. Always carry a knife in case you need to cut the line.

At anchor and not moving, you may be almost impossible to spot. Never assume that other small craft are keeping a good lookout or have more navigational knowledge than you.

CARING FOR THE ENVIRONMENT

The British Canoe Union website contains useful guidelines on the countryside code as does the website of the Scottish Canoe Association.

Kayaks are quiet and unobtrusive, ideal craft to observe wildlife and to discover our natural environment. Everyone can do something to protect or improve the places we enjoy.

Take care not to create a disturbance – keep a reasonable distance from wildlife (if water birds take to the air when you paddle past, then you are too close).

Leave no trace. Ashore it is important that we do not leave our rubbish behind and in many areas this should include our own waste products.

During breeding seasons many creatures may be hidden in the grass or shoreline and it is important to take care when moving about ashore.

If you find discarded fishing lines or other man-made detritus take them with you and dispose of them safely.

LAST WORD

Paddling a sit-on-top is a fantastic way to explore inland and coastal waters. It is a chance to get close to nature and just have fun. Above all else if there is one thing that you should learn from this book, it is the importance of getting some training to help you make wise decisions and stay safe. Sit-on-top kayakers are generally a very hospitable and friendly community. Most kayakers are keen to pass on their knowledge and experience to others.

Take the time to learn more about kayaking to get even more from this great branch of paddle sport. Your sit-on-top brings opportunities for a range of activities from surfing ocean waves to fishing on secluded lakes, and should you choose to specialise in one area, keep hold of your old sit-on-top, you never know when you might want to invite a friend along too.

← **Back of the blade** – The convex face of the paddle, cf. drive face.

← **Beam** – The side of the kayak.

← **Beam sea** – Waves coming from the side.

← **Bow** – The front of the kayak.

← **Break-out** – Move from slow moving water into a faster moving flow of water on a river.

← **Break-in** – Move from fast moving water on a river into slower moving water. Often this is situated behind rocks. See 'eddy'.

← **Broach** – Turning sideways onto the waves. Often occurs involuntarily when paddling in a following sea or through surf.

← **Cadence** – Tempo of a rhythmic movement.

← **Canoe** – A small watercraft in which you kneel (or sit with your legs beneath you) and use a single bladed paddle.

← **Deck** – The top of the kayak.

← **Down drafts** – Wind funnelled down valleys or over cliffs can produce strong gusts of wind.

← **Drive face** – The surface of the paddle which the water is pressing against as you paddle forwards. The concave face of the paddle.

← **Eddy** – Water flowing opposite to the main current. Often seen on a river behind rocks and used as a spot where a kayaker can pause.

← **Feather** – The angle of the paddle blades relative to each other. Unfeathered is used to describe blades set at the same angle (0° feather).

← **Following sea** – Swell or waves which come from behind you.

← **Following wind** – Wind which is coming from behind you. It can feel harder to paddle in a following wind because the kayak will have a tendency to broach.

← **Headland** – An area of the coast that juts out into the sea. Sometimes causing rougher water.

← **Headwind** – Wind blowing directly against you as you paddle along.

← **Hull** – Bottom or underside of the kayak.

← **Hypothermia** – The lowering of the body's core temperature below 37°C. Initial signs are feeling cold and tired, numbness of hands and feet, blue lips and intermittent shivering.

← **Kayak** – A small watercraft in which you sit with your legs in front of you and use a double bladed paddle.

← **Long shore drift** – Many bays have a current moving along the bay parallel to the shore.

← **Overfall** – An area of turbulent water that is caused when a current flows over a shallow area. Similar to a river rapid.

← **Point** – Another name for a headland. Sometimes the cause of rougher water at sea.

← **Portage** – To get out and carry your kayak past a section of river, a flight of locks or over a hill into a lake. This is when a trolley is very handy.

← **Rapid** – Rough water found where the flow of a river is constricted by underwater obstacles such as rocks.

← **Rip current** – A river-like current moving away from the shore. Often found on surf beaches.

← **Sets** – Waves often arrive on a shore in pulses. You will sometimes see surfers just waiting about on the water for the next set of waves to arrive (the notion of the 7th wave being the biggest is not always correct).

← **Shock cord** – Also known as bungee cord. Highly elasticated cord.

← **SOT** – Abbreviation of sit-on-top.

← **Spray deck** (or spray skirt) – nylon or neoprene cover used in decked kayaks to stop water entering the cockpit.

← **Stern** – The rear end of the kayak.

← **Tandem** – A two person kayak.

← **Tidal race** – Area of fast moving and rough water on the sea. This can extend some distance from headlands for instance.

← **Yak** – Abbreviation of kayak. Sometimes used by sit-on-top kayakers to describe the activity.

USEFUL CONTACTS

Instruction and guided tours (the author's company)

Jersey Kayak Adventures

www.jerseykayakadventures.co.uk
Based in Jersey in the Channel Islands. An outfitter running tours and courses for sit-on-top users as well as 'sit-in' sea kayaking around the incredible coastline of Jersey.

National governing bodies & international organisations

British Canoe Union (BCU)

www.bcu.org.uk e-mail info@bcu.org.uk
Represents the interests of all paddlesports at UK and international level. A mine of information, membership includes a British Waterways Licence and third party insurance.

Scottish Canoe Association

www.canoescotland.com

Welsh Canoe Association

www.welsh-canoeing.org.uk

Canoe Association of Northern Ireland

www.cani.org.uk

Australian Canoeing

www.canoe.org.au

Irish Canoe Union

www.canoe.ie

American Canoe Association

www.americancanoe.org

Canadian Recreational Canoeing Association

www.paddlingcanada.com

Federation Quebecoise du canot et du kayak

www.canot-kayak.qc.ca

Fédération Francaise de Canoë-Kayak (FFCK)

www.ffck.org

Professional Association of Diving Instructors (PADI)

www.padi.com
World wide certificated diving courses at all levels with contact details for local dive centres. The site also includes an E-learning module.

British Sub Aqua Club

www.bsac.com
National governing body for dive sports in the UK. Links to local dive centres.

Websites and magazines

www.ukriversguidebook.co.uk
Online river guides (predominantly whitewater, but including touring rivers) covering most of the UK, knowledgebase and forum.

www.ukseakayakguidebook.co.uk
Sister site to the UK Rivers Guidebook. Sea kayaking articles and trip reports from around the UK, with community forum.

www.kayakdiving.com
Mark Theobalds' sit-on-top kayak site contains lots of information about diving from a kayak as well as the opportunity to buy his revised CD-ROM on sit-on-top diving.

www.salzwasserunion.de
German sea kayaking site with a different perspective on sea kayaking in Europe.

www.seapaddler.co.uk
A Jersey-based website for sea kayaking. Contains lots of useful information on skills and techniques.

www.wavelengthmagazine.com
A free west coast American online magazine. Often with sit-on-top tips and kit reviews.

www.kayakfishingstuff.com
Lots of fishing related information and reviews on sit-on-tops at this American site.

www.kayakfishinguk.net
A British sit-on-top kayak fishing resource with an active forum.

www.topkayaker.net
US writer, outfitter and sit-on-top kayaker Tom Holtey's excellent resource centre.

www.kayaksportfishing.com
Some serious fishing and general information at this US site and home to the famous marlin catching story with photos!

Canoe Kayak Magazine
www.canoekayak.com
A US magazine with a range of articles on paddlesport.

Canoe Kayak Magazine (UK)
www.canoekayak.co.uk
British paddlesport magazine with some sit-on-top coverage. A good source for retailers and products.

Kanu Culture magazine
www.kanuculture.com
Australian kayak magazine with a strong Pacific focus with regular features on all types of kayaking and outrigger canoeing.

Books

There are lots of useful books about decked kayaking, along with guides to rivers, lakes and coastal areas. Pesda Press has an extensive catalogue of kayaking books.

Pesda Press LTD
WWW.PESDAPRESS.COM

BCU Canoe and Kayak Handbook
A modern and up-to-date handbook of kayaking and open canoe skills and information.
Editor: Franco Ferrero
ISBN: 09531956-5-1

Kayak Surfing
If you plan to take your kayak into the surf zone, this book will help you get the most out of every wave.
Author: Bill Mattos
ISBN: 09547061-0-2

Sea Kayak Navigation (2nd edition)
Basic and practical navigation skills that are important to know about before you venture onto the sea.
Author: Franco Ferrero
ISBN: 978-1-906095-03-1

Top Tips for Boaters
Practical tips and inspirational ideas gathered by two of the UK's most experienced paddlers and coaches.
Editors: Loel Collins and Franco Ferrero
ISBN: 09547061-4-5

Discover our Hidden Island

Explore Jersey's beautiful coastline
on our modern sit on top kayaks under
the watchful eye of a qualified instructor.

All equipment provided.
No previous experience is needed.
Courses and tours for children and adults
throughout the week and in the school holidays.

JERSEY KAYAK ADVENTURES.co.uk

Ackaless, La Grande Route De La Cote, St. Clement, Jersey JE2 6FW **Telephone: 07797 853 033**

www.jerseykayakadventures.co.uk

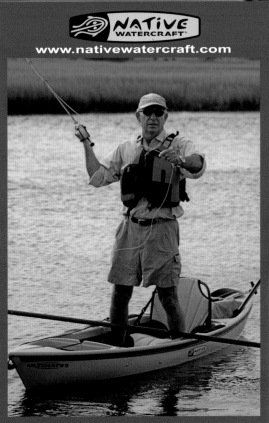

feelfree®

"The Best Feeling On Water"

TRI-YAK   GEMINI   NOMAD   MOVE

For more information visit
www.FeelFreeKayak.com

islander™
K A Y A K S

surf : tour : explore : for playing on rivers, beaches & lakes

 13.5

The fishing sit-on-top

Hula 8.5

The stackable sit-on-top

Paradise II 12.8

The one, two or three person craft

* Paradise II shown fitted with
optional extra Deluxe backrests

For more information & to find your local dealer :

www.islandersitontops.com ... **T: +44 (0)1275 798 100**

islander
K A Y A K S

Which ones yours?

All the best deals on
all brands and accessories
for your sit-on-top kayak.
Mail order direct from our
Nottingham showrooms.

Bon Voyage

the canoe shop   www.desperate-measures.co.uk   tel: 0115 981 6815

De luxe seat

Rod holder

Thigh straps

Taupo Tour

Werner Skagit